Learning to Read, Step by Step!

Ready to Read   Preschool–Kindergarten
• big type and easy words • rhyme and rhythm • picture clues
For children who know the alphabet and are eager to begin reading.

Reading with Help   Preschool–Grade 1
• basic vocabulary • short sentences • simple stories
For children who recognize familiar words and sound out new words with help.

Reading on Your Own   Grades 1–3
• engaging characters • easy-to-follow plots • popular topics
For children who are ready to read on their own.

Reading Paragraphs   Grades 2–3
• challenging vocabulary • short paragraphs • exciting stories
For newly independent readers who read simple sentences with confidence.

Ready for Chapters   Grades 2–4
• chapters • longer paragraphs • full-color art
For children who want to take the plunge into chapter books but still like colorful pictures.

STEP INTO READING® is designed to give every child a successful reading experience. The grade levels are only guides; children will progress through the steps at their own speed, developing confidence in their reading. The F&P Text Level on the back cover serves as another tool to help you choose the right book for your child.

Remember, a lifetime love of reading starts with a single step!

To Rosie —J.M.

This book is dedicated to Joy and George Adamson, who truly believed that all animals are "born free." —S.D.

Special thanks to James G. Doherty, General Curator, Bronx Zoo, Wildlife Conservatory Park.

Text copyright © 1994 by Joyce Milton
Cover art and interior illustrations copyright © 1994 by Silvia Duran

All rights reserved. Published in the United States by Random House Children's Books, a division of Penguin Random House LLC, New York. Originally published in trade paperback in the United States by Penguin Young Readers, an imprint of Penguin Random House LLC, New York, in 1994.

Step into Reading, Random House, and the Random House colophon are registered trademarks of Penguin Random House LLC.

Visit us on the Web!
StepIntoReading.com
rhcbooks.com

Educators and librarians, for a variety of teaching tools, visit us at
RHTeachersLibrarians.com

Library of Congress Cataloging-in-Publication Data is available upon request.
ISBN 978-0-593-43246-4 (trade) — ISBN 978-0-593-43247-1 (lib. bdg.)

Printed in the United States of America
10 9 8 7 6 5 4 3 2 1

This book has been officially leveled by using the F&P Text Level Gradient™ Leveling System.

STEP 3 READING ON YOUR OWN

STEP INTO READING®

A SCIENCE READER

Big Cats

by Joyce Milton
illustrated by Silvia Duran
Random House New York

In Africa the noontime sun is
very hot. A thorn tree is a cool
place for a leopard to take a nap.
But she does not sleep for long.

The leopard is hungry. She sees a herd of zebras. The zebras don't know the leopard is near. The leopard's spots make her hard to see.

Now, quietly, the leopard moves through the tall grass. The zebras sniff the air. Danger is near! They all run.

For one very young zebra,

it is too late.

The leopard drags the
zebra up into the tree.
She will eat it there.

The leopard is a meat-eater. She must hunt to stay alive. Like all cats, leopards are built for hunting. They have sharp teeth.

They have long, hooked claws.
The leopard pushes her claws out
when she attacks. Then she pulls
them back in.

claws out

claws in

Cats can run fast, but they get
tired quickly. Most of the time,
they sneak up on animals. Then
they pounce!

At night it is easier for cats to get close to animals without scaring them away.

So the leopard often sleeps
by day and goes hunting after
sundown. Cats can see in the dark
much better than people can.

Leopards are big cats. Tigers are big cats, too. So are lions and jaguars and cougars and cheetahs.

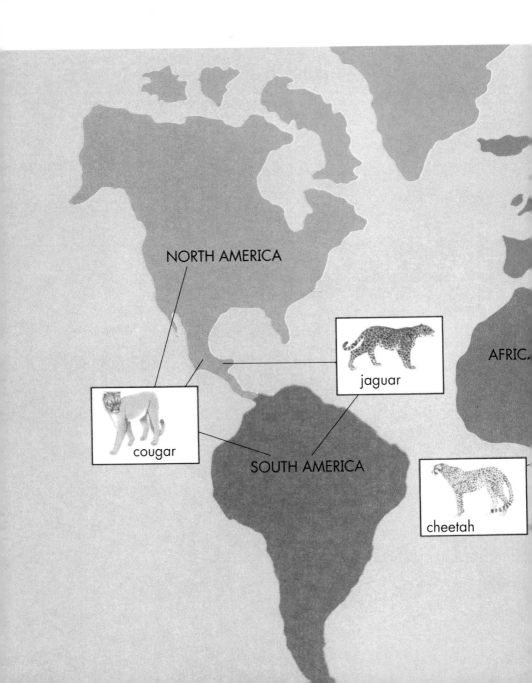

NORTH AMERICA

jaguar

AFRIC.

cougar

SOUTH AMERICA

cheetah

A pet cat usually weighs 10 or 12 pounds. Big cats can weigh hundreds of pounds. This map of the world shows where big cats live.

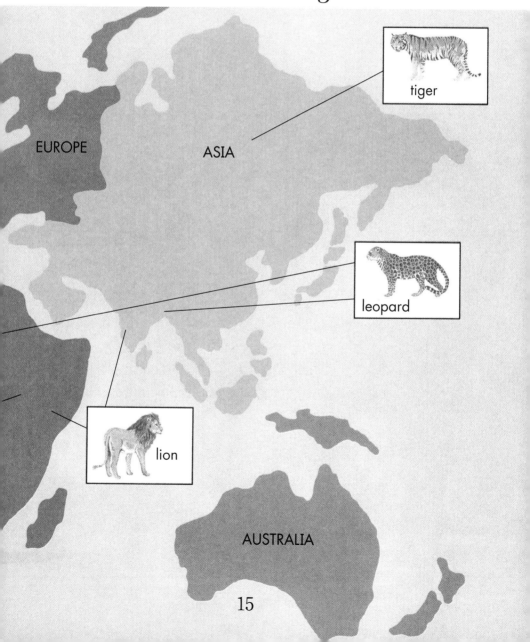

EUROPE

ASIA

tiger

leopard

lion

AUSTRALIA

The biggest big cat in the world is the tiger. A male tiger can weigh up to 600 pounds.

Some tigers can be seven feet long. That's not counting the tail! Most tigers live in the forest. Each tiger has its own hunting ground.

Tigers are very good at hiding.
You might never know one is near.
How can you tell if you are in a
tiger's hunting ground?

You can look for claw marks on
trees. A tiger's claw marks warn
other tigers to keep away.

19

There are many strange and scary stories about tigers. Some say that a man or a woman can turn into a weretiger. Like a werewolf, a weretiger roams the forest at night. It looks for humans to eat. Weretigers are not real.

But a few tigers do become man-eaters. Usually the tigers are too old and sick to catch wild animals anymore. Almost all healthy tigers try to stay away from people.

Most big cats are loners. They live alone. They hunt alone.

But lions enjoy company.
They often live and hunt in
groups called prides.

The male lion has a thick, shaggy mane. That big mane makes it easy for other animals to see the male—and stay out of his way!

Female lions do most of the hunting. The male lion guards the pride and their home. He will fight strange lions. But he would rather scare them off with a loud roar. The lion's roar says: "HERE I AM! THIS IS MY HOME!"

Lions spend most of the day taking it easy. The grown-up lions take catnaps. The cubs pretend to fight one another. But the lion's life isn't always easy.

For part of the year, the plains
are dry. There isn't enough water to
drink. There aren't enough animals
to hunt. Many cubs starve. A lion
has to be strong and lucky
to stay alive.

Most cats don't like to go into the water. But jaguars do. They are very good swimmers. A jaguar will even go fishing. The big cat stands in the river. A fish swims by him.

SMACK! The jaguar hits it hard
with his paw. Fish for dinner!

Jaguars look a
lot like leopards.
But their spots are
different.

leopard

jaguar

There are no lions or tigers in America. But there are cougars. The cougar is the biggest cat found here.

Cougars live in the mountains.
They are great jumpers. Cougar
kittens practice jumping from
rock to rock. The cougar has
other names, too—mountain
lion, puma, or panther.

The cat that is called the black panther is really a leopard.

Every now and then, some leopards give birth to black cubs.

Up close, you can see that a black leopard's fur is spotted. The spots are different shades of black.

The cheetah is another spotted cat. But it looks different from the leopard and the jaguar. It is thinner. Its legs are longer.

Of all the animals in the world,
the cheetah is the fastest. It can run
60 miles an hour—as fast as a car.

Hundreds of years ago, kings
in India kept tame cheetahs
and used them for hunting.

All cats—

from jungle tigers

to pets—

are alike in lots of ways.

Their tongues
are rough, like
sandpaper. They
have sharp teeth
and claws.

39

Pet cats do lots of things that big cats do. They sharpen their claws by scratching.

They love to hunt. Sometimes a kitten will pretend that an old sock is alive, just for the fun of pouncing on it.

Like big cats,
pet cats spend lots
of time licking
themselves clean.

They like to stretch—
just like big cats.

And they love to take catnaps, too.

When a pet cat is happy, it will purr and purr. Do lions and tigers purr? Yes, they do.

Pet cats eat food from the grocery store. This is one big difference between them and big cats.

People take care of pet cats. Big cats have always been able to take care of themselves. But today, that is changing.

Lions, tigers, and other big cats
need wide plains and thick jungles.

But people need land, too. So there is less room for wild animals.

Some countries have set aside
huge parks for wild animals.

Visitors from around the world
come to see the big cats.

Will there be any big cats living free 100 years from now? Yes. But only if we care about saving the big cats' homes.